W9-CIP-525

GIRLSGUIDES

Hangin' Out and Havin' Fun

A Girl's Guide to Cool Stuff to Do

Kristin Ward

the rosen publishing group's
rosen central
new york

Published in 2000 by The Rosen Publishing Group, Inc.
29 East 21st Street, New York, NY 10010

First Edition

Library of Congress Cataloging-in-Publication Data

Ward, Kristin.
    Hangin' out and having fun : a girl's guide to cool stuff to do / by Kristin Ward.
      p.   cm. — (Girls guides)
    Includes bibliographical references and index.
    Summary: Discusses constructive ways for girls in middle school to spend their time.
   ISBN 0-8239-2978-7
   1. Teenage girls—Conduct of life Juvenile literature. 2. Middle school students—Conduct of life Juvenile literature. [1. Conduct of life.] I. Title. II. Series.
   HQ798.W185 1999
   305.235—dc21
                                       99-34083
                                         CIP

Manufactured in the United States of America

Contents

bout This Book

The middle school years are like a roller coaster—wild and scary but also fun and way cool. One minute you're way, way up there, and the next minute you're plunging down into the depths. Not surprisingly, sometimes you may find yourself feeling confused and lost. Not to worry, though. Just like on a roller-coaster ride, at the end of all this crazy middle school stuff, you'll be laughing and screaming and talking about how awesome it all was.

Right now, however, chances are your body is changing so much that it's barely recognizable, your old friends may not share your interests anymore, and your life at school is suddenly hugely complicated. And let's not even get into the whole boy issue. It's a wonder that you can still think straight at all.

Fortunately, reader dear, help is here. This book is your road map. It's also a treasure chest filled with ideas and advice. Armed with this book and with your own inner strength (trust us, you have plenty), you can safely, confidently navigate the twists and turns of your middle school years. It will be tough going, and sometimes you'll wonder if you'll ever get through it. But you—fabulous, powerful, unique you—are up to the task. This book is just a place to start.

So What's the Deal?

What comes to mind when you hear the phrases "having fun" and "hanging out"? Sitting around with your best buds gossiping over raw cookie dough, shopping at the mall, catching a movie with your crush?

Those are all fun things to do, but a whole lot of other things can be fun too. Maybe there are some things you haven't thought of . . . or just haven't thought of as being fun. It might sound a little crazy to think that you could actually have fun figuring out your future, earning money, or bonding with your family. You may be rolling your eyes at the thought that you and your friends can tackle community problems or help change society's view of women while you're hanging out reading magazines or giggling at a slumber party. But it can be done, and it can be fun!

You can move toward achieving your goals

and have fun at the same time. And you can branch out while you hang out. This Girls' Guide is filled with ideas for stuff you can do with your friends, or on your own, that will help you to be a happier and healthier girl today and a stronger and surer woman tomorrow.

It's a Girl's World

At the age of sixteen, Sybil Ludington rode from New York to Connecticut to warn colonists that soldiers of the British army—the dreaded "redcoats"—were moving in to attack Danbury, Connecticut. Although Sybil's ride is less famous than Paul Revere's, she covered almost twice the distance.

Most of all, it's stuff that can be both fun and useful for this wacky, in-between age when you might feel as if you are struggling between being half-girl and half-woman. Here are some ideas and activities that can help you hold on to what is best about being a kid while you build new skills to help you become the woman you want to be.

Of course, no book has all the solutions for making this time in your life easy. No matter how you cut it, the years leading into and through middle school can be an emotional roller coaster. Your body and your brain are changing—a lot. Your emotions can go up and down. It might seem as though your parents do not understand the most important things in your school or social life. Your relationships with other girls, as well as with boys, might be a little rockier than they used to be.

No book can go to school for you or guarantee smooth sailing through adolescence (which is the label society puts on this jumble of physical and emotional changes). But this Girls' Guide can help you make good decisions, maintaining your self-confidence, and find ways to stay in control of who you are and where your life is going. And don't assume that it takes tons of money to have fun or to feel good about yourself. Many activities require only time and thought. A dollar sign ($) is used to indicate your best options for having fun and hanging out on a tight budget.

Along the way, there are also some special features that provide cool info on how other girls and women have stayed focused and confident—and managed to have fun—during crazy times. So take a peek. Check out the ideas. Maybe bring along your Girl's Guide next time you and your buds are having fun and hanging out . . .

Friends and Trends

Lots of new stuff happens in middle school or junior high. You might switch schools, have more home-work, go out on dates, worry more about the future, or feel pressure to have certain clothes or to look a certain way. You and your friends may feel as though you have to keep up with the trends in movies, music, and magazines.

Fads can be fun, but try to keep things in perspective. There are ways to stay hip without losing control of your common sense, your dollars and cents, or your sense of well-being.

Beauty Inside and Out

It's fun to try out new hairstyles, makeup, and nail polish shades with a bunch of buds. But while you are doing each other's hair and nails and seeing how you look in the season's hottest colors, remind one another that you need to develop your inner self as well as your outer self. Take pride in your appearance, but remember that it's just one tiny piece of who you are. Take time to ask

The Buddy System
"I'm really lucky. I have a core group of friends, and I have invested a lot of time in them and in their lives. And no matter what happens, they will always be there for me . . . It's a very reassuring and wonderful thing to know that there is a group of people who care as much about you as they care about themselves."

-Ann Richards, former governor of Texas

yourself and your friends what you can do, rather than buy, to make you feel positive about yourselves.

On the Phone

Chatting on the phone with your best friends is a great stress reliever and usually means lots of laughs, but watch out! If most of your phone time is spent being negative about yourself, other girls, parents and teachers, or what you don't have, stop! Change the conversation to something positive, even for just a few minutes. It's okay to vent, but it's unhealthy not to give the bright side some attention too!

Smart Shoppers

You may enjoy hitting the mall or browsing in cool new boutiques, but shopping can drain both your wallet and your self-confidence. While you and the girls are storming the stores, remind each other that the celebrities and models in magazines, movies, and music videos have teams of experts making them look picture-perfect. Don't spend too much time, energy, or money trying to copy expensive, high-maintenance looks.

Remind yourself that you need to set limits. Make a budget for how much you'll spend on clothes, makeup, and music. Think about other things you might want to save for, like a new piece of furniture for your room, a pet, or a birthday present for a friend.

Time Capsule

With your friends, collect souvenirs of your childhood, hobbies, or time spent with each other. Put everything together in a time capsule. This doesn't have to be some fireproof canister that you bury in the ground for the next generation to dig up. Just a shoebox or Tupperware container will work fine.

Hide it under someone's bed or at the top of a closet. In a few months or years, if the road gets rocky, the time capsule memories will help you regain your sense of security and identity. They can also remind you to hang on to old hobbies and interests, even as you check out new things. Trends come and go, but a talent or activity that you keep working at can bring a lifelong sense of accomplishment.

Ms. Quiz: Female Firsts

Q. Who was the first female artist to have a work commissioned by the U.S. government? What was that work?

A. Near the end of the Civil War, teenage sculptor Vinnie Ream Hoxie had her statue of President Abraham Lincoln placed in the rotunda of the Capitol.

Q. Who was the first woman in American history to receive a medal for performance in combat? What did she do?

A. Lieutenant Jane A. Lombardi was awarded the Air Force Bronze Star for orchestrating a life-saving evacuation of sick and wounded American soldiers from an air base under attack in Da Nang, Vietnam, in 1968.

Q. How old was Queen Christina (1626-1689) when she inherited the throne of Sweden?
A. Six.

Q. Who was the first woman to be elected chief of a major Native American tribe? How long did she serve?

A. Wilma Mankiller was elected chief of the Cherokee Nation in 1985. She held the position until 1994.

Q. Who was the first female prime minister of a Muslim country? What is that country?

A. Benazir Bhutto; Pakistan.

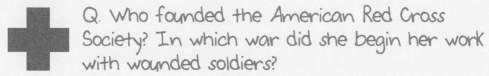

Q. Who founded the American Red Cross Society? In which war did she begin her work with wounded soldiers?

A. Clara Barton; the American Civil War.

Q. What ancient Egyptian queen helped shape the development of Egyptian religious beliefs? (Some historical research suggests that this famous female may even have served as a priest herself, a role traditionally held by men!)

A. Nefertiti.

Q. What was the first coed college in the United States? When was it established?

A. Oberlin College in Oberlin, Ohio, was established in 1833.

Q. Who was the first woman to swim the English Channel? What country was she from?

A. In 1926, New Yorker Gertrude Ederle swam from France to England in fourteen hours and thirty-one minutes.

When cruising the malls or burning up the telephone wires, try to remember that you and your friends are all struggling with new pressures. Help out while you hang out! Keep each other feeling positive and in control, no matter how much pressure you feel to spend on every trend. Remember that the best trend is to be a great friend. That never goes out of style!

Family Matters

When you think of friends, do you picture family members? If not, you might want to think again. Just like your closest pals, family members can be great company. Is it a pain in the neck to have your older sibling be your chaperone? Do you see baby-sitting a younger sibling or visiting an older relative as a chore?

Think of it instead as an opportunity, a chance to get to know someone better—to find out about his or her interests, talents, hopes, and experiences; what you have in common; and what you can learn from each other, just like in any friendship. Here are some ideas for having fun and hanging out with some new friends—whom you've actually known most of your life!

Be a Good Sport

Take in a Little League, high school, college, or professional sports event with your folks, siblings, or grandparents. Rooting for the home team puts you all on the same side to have a good time.

It's a Girl's World

In 1990 Kelly Craig of British Columbia became the first girl to be a starting pitcher in a Little League World Series game. Kelly was the third girl in history to participate in the Little League World Series.

Family Tree $

Involve your whole family in a project to trace your family tree, or genealogy. You and your immediate family can head the project, but use it as a chance to get in touch with faraway relatives and to find out about their lives and families. Tracing your family history is a great way to learn more about your ancestors from the past, the relatives you know today, and even yourself! Keep a scrapbook of your findings, including photos, stories, and interviews—an ongoing story that you can keep adding to.

Team Spirit ▪ ▪ ▪ ▪ ▪ ▪ ➔ $

Organize a sports day to be held once a month with your family and your friends' families. Take turns picking the sport—softball, touch football, volleyball, croquet, tag, bowling, or even just throwing a Frisbee around. Or take a walk around a park or other natural area.

It's a Girl's World

In 1975 Junko Thaei of Japan became the first woman to climb Mount Everest. At 29,028 feet, Everest is the world's tallest mountain.

House of Cards ▪ ▪ ▪ ▪ ▪ ▪ ➔ $

Get the family together to play cards or board games once a week. Take turns picking the games. Give a funny trophy—an old stuffed animal, maybe—to the winner. Whoever wins that week's game gets to keep the trophy until the next week.

Take Our Daughters to Work Day (Ms. Foundation for Women)

Spend a day at an adult's workplace, either through an organized program like Take Our Daughters to Work Day, or just by making a plan with your parent or a friend's parent. You can learn more about the person and about a possible career by "shadowing" him or her on a typical workday.

It's a Girl's World

In the late nineteenth century, Clara Shortridge Foltz and her friend Laura de Force Gordon persuaded California's legislators to change the laws that prevented women from practicing law in that state. Before Foltz and Gordon arrived on the scene, only white males could become lawyers in California.

Cover Girl - - - - - - - - - - - - ➜ $

Go through old photo albums with your parents. Let them tell you about your past, where you were born, and things you liked when you were younger. This will give you a sense of who you are and how you grew into the person you are today. Talking about the experiences that have shaped you can open the door to talking about other things. It might be interesting to share what your view of yourself and the world is now, how it compares to what it used to be, and how and why it is changing.

Encourage your parents and relatives to show you pictures of themselves and their past as well. After all, the experiences that shaped them helped shape you, too.

Culture Vultures

Explore your town or city's cultural and recreational resources—the local museum, theater, park, library, and historical sights. Invite family members on outings. You and your mom could go to an outdoor concert in the park. Is there a museum exhibit that you could visit with your grandparents? Check out a play with your dad. If your folks are going out and you don't want to be stuck at home all day, ask them to drop you and your siblings off at a local historical society, science museum, or library. Hanging out at these places can be a fun alternative to a day of TV reruns.

Everyone in a family is usually busy. Your parents or guardians work, take care of your home, look after you and your siblings, and plan for the future. You and your brothers and sisters have school, homework, extracurricular activities, and friends that you want to spend time with. Work together with family members to plan group outings or special family time. Your school and social life will only become busier as you get older, so take advantage of family time now. Remember, you might meet some of your best friends under your own roof!

What's Cool Out of School

It may seem as if you spend all your waking hours in a classroom, but you probably have a decent amount of free time too—after-school hours, weekends, holidays, and summer break.

Do you and your buds use that time wisely? Sure, sometimes it's great to relax, watch old movies, chill out to your favorite tunes, or hunt down bargains at the mall. But do you and the gang do the same old things all the time? Are you sick of going to the same stores? Starting to notice that the articles in your favorite magazines are pretty much the same each month? Why not make free time quality time?

Getting Extracurricular

Sports are a great way to exercise, learn about healthy competition, and become part of a team.

If you don't make a school team, don't be discouraged. Play a sport outside of school. If you don't like sports, try something else—drama club, student government, the school newspaper, chorus, band, or a special-interest science, video, or language club. Be open-minded. Try whatever appeals to you. Use it as a chance to make new friends. Investigate classes and clubs that are available in your community.

It's a Girl's World

Figure skater Sonja Henie of Norway first won the Norwegian National Skating championship at age ten. She was eleven when she participated in the Olympics for the first time. Henie is the only skater ever to win gold medals in three consecutive Olympics.

The Buddy System

"I was twelve years old when I discovered that toast didn't have to be white bread. I was sleeping over at my best friend, Laurie's, house when I first smelled the sharp aroma of rye toast. I was astonished and laughed at her outrageousness; she was toasting RYE BREAD. Then she made me taste it, and I was hooked.

"This was only one small way my best friend has broadened my horizons, and that's one of the things best friends do best."

–Valerie Schultz on her friendship with Laurie, which began in third grade

Food for Thought

Cook up some fun in the kitchen. The main ingredients? Some friends and a couple of cookbooks. Pick out a few recipes—choose healthy snacks or meals if you're worried about staying healthy and fit. Try a new recipe once every couple of weeks, and before long you'll have a whole menu to pick from.

Talent Show

Plan a low-key talent show, with yourself and your friends and family as the performers and audience. Nothing fancy—just pick a date and a spot. Draw names from a hat to figure out the order of performers. Sing, act, juggle, dance, or read an original poem or short story. What better way is there to get comfortable presenting yourself to a group?

It's a Girl's World

At the age of sixteen, Sacagawea, a Native American woman of the Shoshone tribe, played an invaluable role as a guide for Lewis and Clark's famous Voyage of Discovery. This journey took the explorers from St. Louis, Missouri, to the Pacific Northwest between 1805 and 1807.

Book Club

Meet once a month with your buddies to chat about a book you've all read. You could pick themes for your book club, like biographies of famous women. It's great if there's some gossip and giggles, but try to spend a little time discussing the book, too. Book club Web sites on the Internet contain lots of good ideas about how to organize book clubs, including discussion questions for certain books.

It's a Girl's World

Canadian-born Mary Pickford started her career onstage at age five. At the age of sixteen, she became a box office hit in silent films. Involved in film production and distribution as well as performing, Mary Pickford became the motion picture industry's first millionaire.

Reaching Out While Hanging Out

free Tibet

Do you and your friends spend a lot of time complaining about problems—problems with your school, your community, your world? Everyone needs to vent and get things off her chest. But you can do more than just feel gloomy or powerless. Take the next step. Don't talk only about problems; talk about solutions!

Volunteer – – – – – – – → $

Check out volunteer opportunities in your community. Find out about organizations that work with the elderly, the sick, or the physically or mentally challenged.

One of the best ways to get perspective on your own problems is to learn about the problems of others. Volunteering is also a way to actually do something about a problem that worries or troubles you. Many organizations can use your help. You can start by calling local hospitals, environmental groups, literacy groups, or animal shelters. They may have volunteer work for you or be able to point you in the direction of an organization that does.

Brainstorm - - - - - - - → $

If you and the gals are hanging out on a rainy day or lazing around at a slumber party and you need to stir things up a bit, grab a notebook, open your mind, and brainstorm a list of problems in your school or community.

Think of creative ways you can contribute to solutions. Troubleshooting and problem solving are skills that you will always need in school, relationships, and jobs. And getting things done can be a lot of fun. Who knows? Your rainy-day ideas might turn into satisfying projects that give you a chance to do something for your community.

It's a Girl's World
In 1957, Elizabeth Eckford, age fifteen, and MinnieJean Brown, age sixteen, were among the nine black students who integrated Little Rock High School in Little Rock, Arkansas. An angry mob tried to prevent the students from entering the school, and President Dwight D. Eisenhower had to send in the National Guard to maintain peace.

Girl Talk $

Feeling frustrated by all the images of stick-thin models or pictures of women in bikinis that are used to sell everything from cars to jewelry?

Don't just swallow your frustration! Start a conversation with your girlfriends. Talk to each other about how girls and women are treated in society today, especially in the media. Keep a group journal. Take turns jotting down notes when you and your friends talk about issues facing girls and women. Your observations and conversations are more than thoughtful—they are powerful. They represent the concerns, dreams, and plans of a whole new generation of women!

Go, Girl!

"Don't get stuck in a rut and close yourself off. No one has just one gift. Sometimes it takes a struggle to find out what those other gifts are."
—Lindsay Milasich, age fourteen, after realizing that she did not have the right body type to fulfill her childhood dream of becoming a ballerina

Sisterhood

Maybe you would like to connect with other girls outside your immediate circle of friends. Start a girls' newsletter with neighborhood, camp, school, or long-distance friends. Include pen pals from another country so that you can compare experiences. Ask a foreign-language teacher at your school for suggestions on finding international pen pals. Starting a newsletter will take a little time and organization. You might need to save up some money—from raking leaves, baby-sitting, or other chores you do to earn spending cash—since there will be costs for paper, photocopying, and postage.

At times, you may feel that you don't have much control over your life. It may seem as though parents, teachers, or older siblings have all the power and make all the decisions that affect you. But you and your friends have the ability to do a lot of good things for yourself, each other, and your community. You have been hanging out with your buddies for years. Now try reaching out with them!

It's a Girl's World

When her husband couldn't handle running the family printing business, Mary Katherine Goddard took charge. She ran the shop in Baltimore, Maryland, that printed the Declaration of Independence in 1776. In addition to her success as a printer, Goddard served as postmaster of Baltimore, which also distinguishes her as the first woman to have a job in the federal government.

Boy, Oh, Boy!

Have some of your buddies started to make noise about boys? Are boys all they seem to talk or think about?

Maybe that's how you are beginning to feel too. Maybe you can't get enough of the preteen and teen magazines that are filled with hints and tips about crushes and dates. There is no right or wrong way to feel. Some girls start getting interested in guys, dates, and romance around the middle school years. But some girls don't care about the whole girl/guy scene until much later.

Wherever you are when it comes to crushes

and dating, here are two helpful tips: First, don't put yourself in a situation that makes you uncomfortable. And second, your body is just that—*your* body—so you set the limits. Remind yourself that there is no set schedule for first kisses or first boyfriends. Every girl is different and moves at her own pace. If you want some fun, low-pressure ways to hang out with a crush, here are a few ideas:

Dinner and a Movie ···········▶

There is nothing wrong with this old favorite!

Supper Party

You and your crush could try to cook dinner for a group of friends. It's a good idea to make sure that your parents are at home (or his folks, if you cook the feast at his house) in case there is a catastrophe in the kitchen and you need a hand. You can ask parents to help you keep the cooking and eating area off-limits to siblings.

Fun and Games

Go out with a bunch of friends—bowling, biking, and in-line skating are fun group activities. Group picnics and ice-skating parties can be fun too!

That's the Ticket − − − − − − − − − − − −

For a special occasion, make plans in advance. You might need to save up some money and order tickets ahead of

time. Pick a concert by a singer or band you both like, or catch a play or sports event.

The Buddy System

"We're best friends for the long haul. In fact, one of the jokes we have is what color our hair will be when we're seventy. Karlene's blond, so we figure she'll be platinum by then. I want to have jet-black like Morticia Addams."

-Julia Louis-Dreyfus, actress, talking about her best friend

The dating scene can be overwhelming. It can also be tough if you start dating earlier or later than your close friends. Try to be supportive and understanding of each other. Just as you have to balance schoolwork and extracurricular activities, and family and friends, you have to make adjustments when there is a new person in your life or in a friend's life. You have been through too much with your girlfriends to let crushes crush your friendship!

Is Your Body on Your Mind?

7

Have you become more critical of the way you look lately? Maybe you've started to wonder if boys think you are pretty, if your friends think you are pretty, if you think you are pretty. In our culture we seem to make a big deal out of how people look. Movies, magazines, music videos, and TV shows are filled with beautiful people. Advertising tries to make people think that they will be prettier or more popular or happier if they just buy a certain product.

Getting hit with such messages all the time can be confusing, even hurtful. How are you supposed to feel if you don't look like the people in the advertisements?

It can be really tough around the middle school years, when your body and feelings might seem out of control already. You may feel impossibly far away from the seemingly perfect, put-together faces and lives that you are constantly seeing on television and at the newsstand. You might feel pressure to go on a diet, get a certain haircut, or buy expensive clothes and makeup in order to fit in or be popular.

The truth is that none of these things will make you happy. Happiness comes from confidence and feeling good about who you are, not how you look. Sure, it's nice to know that you look good, but the best way to look good is to stay healthy and happy. Beauty starts inside!

Balancing Act

Try meditation or yoga to keep your head clear and your mind calm. Think about the difference between real and ideal. These lines often get blurred in the media. A lot of time and money is spent on clothing, makeup, and hairstylists for celebrities and models. Expensive lighting and photography equipment is also used. What you see in magazines and movies is an ideal setting, a fantasy. In the real world, without all the time, money, and fancy equipment, a different kind of beauty exists.

Quiet Time

It's great to hang out with your circle of friends, but it is also okay to take some quiet time just to read, rest, or relax by yourself. You'll have more energy and attention for your friends when you are together if you make sure to take care of your own needs when you are apart.

Exercise

Pick sports or activities that you enjoy so you will be more likely to stick to a routine that keeps you fit and active. Use your body; don't abuse it! And remember, exercise can take many forms. It doesn't have to be a workout at the gym. You can go dancing with your friends or put on your favorite music and dance around your own room. You can go hiking, enjoy a long bike ride, or even just take a walk.

It's a Girl's World
Wilma Rudolph overcame childhood polio to win three gold medals at the 1960 Olympic Games as a member of the U.S. Track Team.

Good Nutrition

Try to eat a healthy, balanced diet. If you are confused about what this means, unsure about what is healthy for your age and build, or afraid that you are going to eat too much and gain weight, ask your parents to set up an appointment with a nutritionist or dietitian.

Eating right doesn't have to be guesswork. Get the facts you need to make healthy choices about eating and exercise. If you want to keep looking your best, you have to eat the kinds and amounts of foods that will keep you feeling your best.

Religion

The world does not consist of just physical things. Explore your spiritual side too. Trying to figure out how you fit in to the "big picture" of life can help you gain perspective. It may make your immediate, everyday problems seem small.

Self-Defense

Classes in the martial arts or other forms of self-defense offer great exercise for the body and mind. Such classes have become increasingly popular in the last few years and are available in most areas.

Punching Bag

If the pressure to look or act a certain way starts to get you down, don't take it out on yourself. But don't keep it inside either. Hang a punching bag somewhere in your house or visit a gym that has one. Take your anger and frustration out on the punching bag. Let the bag take the blows, not your self-confidence.

Take a Walk

If school sports are too high pressure but you are concerned about staying in shape, start a walking club with some friends. You can walk after school or on the weekends. And of course you can walk and talk at the same time, so you can catch up while you work out!

It's a Girl's World

In 1985 Libby Riddles became the first woman to win the Iditarod, Alaska's famous dogsled race.

Every woman or girl is beautiful in her own way. You have to learn to appreciate your good points, accept the things you're not so thrilled with, and then move on to more important things. Do not waste too much energy on what you see in the mirror. That could be anybody. Your personality, the special qualities that make up the unique person that is you, is inside your heart and head. It doesn't show up in mirrors or on scales!

Shape Your Future

8

You may spend a great amount of time these days thinking of how you look or how you want to look. It is healthy to focus on something different. Try thinking about what you might like to do or be in the future instead of how you might like to look.

You have lots of time ahead of you to figure out what you want to do with your life, and you certainly don't have to get it all nailed down right now. Still, it never hurts to do some dreaming, learning, and even planning.

If you develop a clearer sense of where you want to end up, you can start heading in that direction. Middle school is a good time to begin asking yourself not only where you want to go in life but also how you are going to get there. And of course, you and your pals can be thinking about the future even while you're hanging out.

Stat Chat

There were 328 girls among the 955,000 high school football players in the 1994–95 school year.

Three hundred women attended the first Women's Rights Convention in Seneca Falls, New York, in 1848. The convention kicked off the women's movement and the fight for a woman's right to vote.

In the United States, there are 67 female managers or administrators for every 100 men working in similar high-authority jobs. In Japan the figure is 9 out of 100.

Worldwide there are more female than male students in higher education (colleges, universities, and graduate schools).

Approximately half of the students in law school are women. In medical school, female students are the majority!

In the United States today, 75 percent of girls finish high school. In 1970 only about 53 percent completed high school.

Currently in the United States, men greatly outnumber women in such fields as engineering and computer science.

Just one out of every six engineering degrees goes to a woman, and women earn only one out of every three computer science degrees.

Dollars and Sense

After-school or weekend jobs can be a great way to earn money. Learning new skills, taking responsibility, and earning your own money are all things that help develop your sense of independence.

You say that you can't find a job that appeals to you? Get creative. You and your friends could start your own business. Look around; ask questions.

It's a Girl's World

Twelve-year-old Kelly Moser runs her own business, which she calls Kelly's Pins. She designs and sells friendship pins with the colors and patterns of different countries' flags. Kelly started the business when she was eight, and she donates some of her profits to charity.

Can you walk pets when neighbors are away? (You might want to do this in pairs for safety, rather than heading to an empty house on your own.) Could you set up tutors for kids at school? Is someone needed to sell snacks and beverages at school sports events?

Find a need in your school or neighborhood, then figure out a way to fill it. It is never too early to start developing your business skills, instincts, and knowledge. To get ahead in business, you have to have a head for business!

Ready, Set, Internet!

Today is definitely the information age, so it is a great idea to get comfortable and current with the technology that can help you access and process information. Being able to find reliable information fast will help you with schoolwork, college planning, and even job searches. So surf the Net! Learn how to use this resource safely and efficiently. One fun way to practice using the Internet is to set up scavenger hunts that you and your pals can go on in cyberspace. Take turns picking cool topics—a celebrity, an athlete, a country that you are curious about—then see what comes up from different Web sites and links. Using the Internet for fun will make it a breeze later on when you want to use it for school assignments.

Higher Education and Cool Destinations

Investigate colleges, careers, internships, and places you would like to visit. Each of your friends can pick a few colleges, destinations, or organizations.

Split up to do some detective work on your own.

Write or call for brochures and information; surf the Internet; and talk to teachers, older siblings, or parents. Then you and your friends can pool all your information at a pizza party!

You might discover some useful things. Maybe you're dying to go to France—that's an incentive for taking up French at school. Do you want to go to college in an area where skiing is available? Maybe you should start setting money aside for great ski equipment. (Hey, at least you'll have enough for a cool ski trip, whether or not you end up chilling at a college by the slopes.)

Role Models

Get together with friends and make a list of women role models. Talk about and research women you admire. Learn how they became successful. What steps did they take to reach their goals? What might you need to do, think about, or work on to follow in their footsteps?

Present Tense

Sure, it's great to think about the future, but don't let it overwhelm you. Remember to appreciate where you are right now, too. Don't get so wrapped up in the future that you forget to enjoy the present.

Do not be afraid to talk with your friends if you have concerns about the immediate or distant future. It's natural to worry about what high school will be like, how starting to date more will affect your friendships, if you will be able to keep your grades up, or if you will have a good social life.

The Buddy System
"We have fun together; we help each other; but, above all, it is our talking that makes my life fuller. With my friend I can reveal more of myself than I do with most other people: my uncertainties, my observations, my achievements. Beyond sharing the highs and lows of life, we share the details, the ordinary stuff."

—Katherine Canfield, editor and mother

Maybe you're even starting to think about how you'll make decisions about things like college, marriage, and careers.

Once you put your worries on the table, try to think of strategies and support systems that you and your friends can use to tackle those worries. Work together to change your mind-set from scared to prepared!

bonding Forming a close relationship with a person through spending lots of time together and sharing common interests and concerns.

boundaries Limits set to protect yourself both physically and emotionally.

budget A plan for how you earn, save, and spend money over set periods of time.

crush Intense but often short-lived attraction to, or obsession with, someone who interests you romantically.

fad A style or activity that becomes very popular among a lot of people for a short period of time.

gender A sexual category such as male or female.

genealogy Family history.

goal Something you want to achieve.

identity Features and characteristics of your personality that make you a unique individual.

inner self The thoughts and feelings that you do not show to the outside world.

middle school A period in your education that goes from fifth or sixth grade through eighth or ninth grade.

outer self The thoughts, feelings, and actions that you show to the outside world.

pressure The force or stress felt when you have to do something hard or unpleasant, or when you have to get something done by a certain time or in a certain way that you are not sure you can do.

self-confidence Being comfortable with who you are and what you do.

stress Anxiety or tension felt when you are under a lot of pressure or are feeling nervous or overwhelmed.

vent To let yourself get really emotional about something so you can then calm down and figure out how to deal with it rationally.

volunteer To do some work or help someone as an act of kindness, not to earn money.

It's a Girl's World: *helpful info*

Association for Women in Science
1200 New York Avenue NW, Suite 650
Washington, DC 20005
(800) 886-2947
Web site: http://www.awis.org

4-H Council
7100 Connecticut Avenue
Chevy Chase, MD 20815
(301) 961-2840
Web site: http://www.fourhcouncil.edu

Girl Scouts of the U.S.A.
420 Fifth Avenue
New York, NY 10018-2798
(212) 852-8000
Web site: http://www.gsusa.org

International Center for Research on Women
1717 Massachusetts Avenue NW
Washington, DC 20036
(202) 797-0007
Web site: http://www.icrw.org

Take Our Daughters to Work Day
Ms. Foundation for Women
120 Wall Street, Thirty-third Floor
New York, NY 10005
(800) 676-7780
Web site: http://www.ms.foundation.org

Bauermeister, Erica. *500 Great Books by Women: A Reader's Guide.* Des Moines, IA: Meredith Books, 1998.

Canfield, Jack. *Chicken Soup for the Teenage Soul: 101 Stories of Life, Love, and Learning.* New York: Heath Communications, 1997.

Felder, Deborah G. *The 100 Most Influential Women of All Time: A Ranking Past and Present.* Secaucus, NJ: Citadel Press, 1998.

Jukes, Mavis. *It's A Girl Thing: How to Stay Healthy, Safe, and in Charge.* New York: Knopf, 1996.

Lunardini, Christine. *What Every American Should Know About Women's History: 200 Events That Shaped Our Destiny.* Holbrook, MA: Adams Media Corp., 1996.

Madaras, Lynda. *What's Happening to My Body?: A Book for Girls: A Growing Up Guide for Parents and Daughters.* New York: Newmarket Press, 1987.

McCoy, Sharon. *50 Nifty Super Friendship Crafts.* Los Angeles: Lowell House, 1997.

Odean, Kathleen. *Great Books for Girls: More Than 600 Books to Inspire Today's Girls and Tomorrow's Women.* New York: Ballantine Books, 1997.

Page, Cristina. *The Smart Girl's Guide to College: A Serious Book Written by Women in College to Help You Make the Perfect College Choice.* New York: Noonday Press, 1997.

Index

Credits

About the Author

Kristin Ward is a children's book editor and manager at a school library publishing house in New York City. In her free time, she enjoys theater, running, and hanging out and having fun in the Big Apple!

Photo Credits

Cover photo, pp. 9, 14, 21, 27, 32 by Scott Bauer; pp. 15, 40, 43 by John Bentham.

Series Design

Laura Murawski

Layout

Oliver Rosenberg